The Art of my Heart by Chirag Parmar

Copyright © Chirag Parmar, 2020

All rights reserved. No part of this book should be repeated, scanned or transmitted in any form without the expressed written consent of the author, Chirag Parmar.

All content, including title, have been written by Chirag Parmar.

ISBN: 9798688714296

This book is dedicated to my life thus far, to those who helped me up after getting knocked down & to those who never gave up on me.

Contents

Be better but stay you — 5
The Masterplan — 7
Nam-jai — 9
One More Day — 11
Wrong Places — 13
Never Stop — 15
Beside you — 17
Hope — 19
All of me — 21
A Dangerous Game — 23
Blind — 25
Sense — 27
Rule — 29
The Fear — 31
Muse — 33
At First Sight — 37
Saudade — 39
Sometimes — 41
Sehnsucht — 45
Hamartia — 47
All in the math — 49
Elemental — 51
You have — 53
When World's Collide — 55
Pain Perseverance Promise — 59
Querencia — 61

Be better but stay you

Some days I wake up and know where I want to be
   how I'm going to get there, being better but staying me
other days I wake up feeling sluggish and slow
   oh so depressed, feeling so damn low
the hardships I've faced, the pain just pours
   the strain on my family, just want to scream no more
accidents, arguments and tears are aplenty
   had enough for a lifetime and I'm only in my twenties
but better days are coming because my circle is strong
   I've learnt from my mistakes and from now can do no wrong
choosing wisely in words, friends and choices
   blocking out the evil and all the irrelevant noises
following my heart, wary of my gut, and listening to my mind
   all 3 combined will surely lead me to happiness of some kind
striving to achieve a feeling that's ethereal
   beyond mind, body, soul and anything physical
calculating and educating my mind with the truth
   choosing not to entertain it with the lies and bull
I lost my heart in the worst kind of way
   but great people gave me pieces of theirs so I could rebuild my own
with this new heart I will be better
   be better, but stay me.

The Masterplan

Caught up in my own world thought it was about me
I was living in my dreams a real-life escapee
perhaps it was God's plan or part of His strategy
to bring me crashing down with the worst type of tragedy
I was left broken, my heart open for everyone to see
but then like a light guiding my path, they appeared – my family
now, after some time, the pain is just a memory
my life is like Schubert's no. 8 unfinished symphony
it encapsulates all feelings like a heartfelt melody
at present incomplete but fulfilment is down to me
it will flourish over time and, hopefully, end happily.

Nam-jai

If I made each rainbow end where you stand
so that you could see the true treasure is your life itself

If I made the stars fall like snow
glisten and transform the landscape into a canvas for your imagination

If I made your problems weightlessness like space
float like bubbles for you to pop and watch dissipate

If I made the moon's light purify your soul
to open your heart to your limitless possibilities

If I made each season of pain and sorrow
change to that of pleasure and beautiful tomorrows

If I were to lay each brick to pave the way of your journey for every single mile
would you spare a smile?

One more day

If I had one more day
then all day we would play.
If I had one more day
for your best I would pray.
If I had one more day
then everything I have wanted to, I would say.
If I had one more day,
from the pain I would take you far away.
If I had more day
I would give you the most beautiful bouquet.
If I had one more day
all the love I've kept hidden I would convey.
If I had one more day
I would help you find your way.
If I had one more day
then this day would replay.

Wrong Places

I'm looking for the light in the darkest of umbra's
I'm looking for my path on a road already travelled
I'm looking for a reason in a pool full of excuses
I'm looking for a way through, through a library of failed methods
I'm looking for absolute happiness from things that are relative
I'm looking for myself outside of me.

I'm looking for help from the masters of deceit
I'm looking for loyalty from accomplices of treachery
I'm looking for the truth from those born to lie
I'm looking for love from those who use it as a means to an end
I'm looking for my soul in a maze I created.

Never Stop

Maybe life isn't for me I'm always hard hit
it feels like a puzzle but I can't seem to fit
My world is like a rubik's cube it's too complex
all the good that I do seems to have bad effects
Sleep to me is both a friend and a foe
helps me to rest but not to let things go
My nightmares bleed into reality unsure which way is up
always on edge, at any time I could erupt
I'm trying to write my life; my life isn't going to write itself
but sometimes I feel like there's a puppet master pulling my strings in stealth
Feels like I'm playing a game, perhaps the game is playing me
or am I simply on God's chessboard as a pawn piece
I'm doing all I can to make myself a name
but I'm merely a cub, I've yet to earn my mane
Don't know what to do my life feels like a battlefield
but it's me against my inner demons I cannot afford to yield
The weight of my care is pressing down hard
my experiences are visible on all of my scars
Life will try to knock me down into a pit
but with an eternal fire my spirit is lit
My soul will not quit.

Beside you

When we've bled the knowledge from all the books
and muted all the notes in songs

When we've eaten all the animals
and the planet is ready to consume us

When planes are falling like flies
and cars are being crushed like ants

When we've drowned the land
and dried up all the seas

When we've suffocated nature
and find ourselves finding it hard to breathe

When hell erupts through the earth
and our sins block our path to heaven

When the sun is blocked by our darkness
and our inner demons begin to shine

When the starry sky has lost its sparkle
and the planet's core has its one last beat

When everyone around have lost their minds
and mankind is lost for eternity

When lifetimes flash by in a manner of minutes
and the end of days is only seconds away
Who would you want beside you?

Hope

They say without food a person would last up to 3 weeks
They say without sleep a person would last 2 weeks
They say without water a person would last up to 3 days
They say without oxygen a person could last 3 minutes

But without hope?
I pray I never find out.

All of me

I cannot give you the world but I can make you mine
I cannot give you a huge house, only a warm loving home
I cannot give you a fancy car, just the drive of your life
I cannot give you expensive jewellery but I can give you my most prized possessions
I cannot give you a bottomless supply of money, just infinite moments to be cherished
I cannot give you the best man in the world, just the best I can be
I see the God in you and want to worship you
I see the human in you and want to love you
In this life, and all that follow, be mine because I'm forever yours.

A Dangerous Game

What if,
perhaps
one day
soon,
maybe
eventually
someday

I'll stop with later.

Blind

Oh, how I weep for the dreamer without an imagination.

He sees the night sky but not the stars that burn bright
He sees roses blossom but cannot smell the sweet scent
He sees the sun shine but cannot feel the warmth of the rays
He sees the movement of life but is frozen inside a moment
He sees places of worship but cannot understand hope & faith
He sees laughter and smiles but knows not happiness
He sees the world's injustices but cannot be its saviour
He knows what's right but all he does seems to turn out wrong
He knows what he wants but it's not his to have
He knows what home is but it's the only place he can't find.

Sense

Can you see the sand pass through my heart like an hourglass
as each pump of blood is a moment of life passed
Can you taste the bittersweet victories my heart has won
when its sown itself up after the seams became undone
Can you smell the fear as my heart flies into the unknown
as each beat recalls the turbulence of the path, so far, flown
Can you feel the 808 beat of my heart intensify
as all possible futures collide with each version I try to justify
Can you hear the stories and poems of my heart
as it hopes to live on, even after it departs.

Rule

There is only one rule governed by time
There will be an end to every lifeline
Everything in-between is just a grey area
An opportunity to leave a legacy lasting forever.

The Fear

A spark that ignites into flames
your body screams as if it were in pain
the muscles in your body begin to tense
every breath of air suddenly becomes dense
your mind can't function your thoughts are renegade
your voice seems lost, your words have runaway
the cocooned butterflies try to escape
out of your stomach the nervousness exacerbates
hot lava courses through your veins
once clear now cloudy your judgement begins to wane
your savage heart beats against the ribcage
legs feel weak will you make it to the stage
your palms start sweating you're beginning to lose your grip
others can see it from the trembling of your lip
the weight of the pressure bears down on your shoulders
you're trying your best but can't hold your composure
your insecurities like a hurricane take you off track
memories of past failures like thunder and lightning flashback
the devil inside is rooting for your failure
the angel's voice has disappeared where is your saviour?
will you surrender to what could happen and repent for eternity
or flourish and fly in what could be & be free for eternity?

Muse

Do you think its paved
the path that you 'choose'
Do you think it's up to you
if you win or lose

Are all people same
with equal opportunities
Can some be more
than just liabilities

Does money buy happiness
or just an easy life
Have you really lived
if you've never had to survive

Does fear control our future
making us stutter at the doors of opportunity
Maybe it's just a question of courage
to allow us to master our own destiny

Do people know what trust really is
or is its 'losing a value' a danger
You can't trust those closest to you
but can confide in a total stranger

Is love really selfless
or selfishness disguised
Does it set you free
or freedom, it denies

Do travellers want to see the world
or just follow their heart's song
Are they wandering aimlessly
or finding a place to belong

Are we a rubik's cube to be solved
or a puzzle to be completed
If we remain beautifully broken
does that mean that we're defeated

Are masks only for show
to wear to parties and masquerades
Are they used to hide our true self
or to deceive and betray

Are we all puppets on strings
controlled by the ghosts of our past
Is our life just a big stage in a box
for all to look in through the glass

Does religion bring us together
or does our pride in it divide us
Does God really exist or are they 'fictional hope'
maybe hope in humanity is all we need to guide us

Does forever last an eternity
or does it come with an expiration date
Do people promise eternity blindly
and then blame it onto fate

Why is the end embedded in us from the beginning
as if life is measured by pre-determined milestones
Maybe we need to go back to the start and focus on the journey
making every moment count, building a story so legendary
it's hard to believe.

At First Sight

Wind changed direction
fate changed plans
she went left
right into me
her curves silhouetted
my body rigid
her eyes sparkled
my mind mesmerised
her hips swayed
my eyes fixated
her hair flowed
my knees trembled
her eyelids fluttered
my thoughts fumbled
her smile; captivating
my soul caught.

Time went on
the moment frozen
my heart melted.

Saudade

How dark the days
when all I can do is miss you.
How bright the nights
when in my dreams I'm with you.

Sometimes

Sometimes the end can be the start
Sometimes growing means first falling apart

Sometimes playing it safe holds you back
Sometimes a risk can get you back on track

Sometimes time can wear you down
Sometimes a moment can turn it all around

Sometimes a smile hides your fears
Sometimes joy can flow through tears

Sometimes pain can be a blessing in disguise
Sometimes you think you're unworthy so happiness you deny

Sometimes nothing is all you need
Sometimes it's hard to distinguish between need and greed

Sometimes being surrounded is the loneliest place to be
Sometimes being alone doesn't mean you're lonely

Sometimes the silence can be quite deafening
Sometimes chaos can be tranquilising

Sometimes you do things you know you're not allowed
Sometimes you do things to make your parents proud

Sometimes it seems the odds aren't on your side
Sometimes you just have to let fate decide

Sometimes all you can offer is not enough
Sometimes you've got to push past giving up

Sometimes love is nothing more than a feeling
Sometimes it can be as important as breathing

Sometimes remembering why you started will see you through
Sometimes you just need to believe in you.

Sehnsucht

I miss the smiles of faces I have yet to see
       the touch of people yet to meet
       the memories that are waiting to happen
       gifts that I have yet to treat.

I miss the nights I can't remember
       places yet to go
       happiness yet to be felt
       the sacrifices yet to forego.

I miss the lessons learnt from pending mistakes
       the hope from perils unknown
       the pain of working towards dreams yet had
       a place to rest in my house yet to turn home.

I miss the heart of the woman yet to love
       the laughter of my children yet to call me dad
       silly times like a family pile-up
       family portraits yet to be had.

Hamartia

Infinite futures lay before my feet
every moment has led to this, there is no retreat
past, present & future all collide in the moment
the pain, perseverance & promise, I am my only opponent.

This change is demanded and life has forced me to choose
call it fate or God's plan, but this is it, all or nothing, win or lose
consequences, direction, cause & effect
my brain's crunching numbers, trying to protect.

The world moves slowly, time is stood still
my mind is pacing rapidly, trying to figure out my true will
what's right, what's wrong, the line begins to blur
even my thought process begins to slur.

Mind and heart, fatigued, go toe to toe
it's the final round, what will be, who truly knows
once the hero of my story, recovering from battles lost & won
an all-consuming & relentless world, has all the good become undone?

The path chosen to date has led me to this pinnacle
one last hurdle to overcome, the future has become unthinkable
come what may, the decision is in my hands
let it be known, I was who I am.

All in the math

The laws of life can sometimes be interpreted through many theories
each theory symbolising a personal experience; their life story.
Life can feel like algebra, hard to understand
no matter how hard you try to calculate the vector it can still get out of hand.
It's unavoidable, somehow, you'll deviate from the path
a simple miscalculation can leave you broken in the aftermath.
The forecast for the future can't always be accurately measured
but you've got to avoid using past memories for your time series method.
The data you have will always be incomplete
variables are constantly changing and finding a balance is no easy feat.
You've got to differentiate between the good and the bad
subtract the negativity and multiply all that, for which you are glad.
Find the correlation between what you do and happiness
formulate a plan to avoid all that makes you stress.
Look for trends in experiences to guide your journey
maybe the solution is just to live life freely.

Elemental

Waves reach for the shore for her lover's hand
the moon shines its light at night in search for his
volcanoes erupt with the power of love
the sun's warmth; lover's arms and gentle kisses.

The earth moves to be closer to its one and only love
the wind calls out their lover's name
trees grow; a love flourishing over time
thunder and lightning strike like a love untamed.

Tornadoes & hurricanes dance like lovers moving in unison
stars, guiding their love home, shining brightly at night
forests firmly grounded by roots, lovers intertwined for eternity
the silence a tranquillity, when lovers finally unite.

You have

You have
comfort in your smiles
wisdom in your words
gentleness in your touch
kindness in your eyes
faith in your thoughts
courage in your actions
firmness in your beliefs
bravery in your personality
intellect in your mind
craftsmanship in your hands
enthusiasm in your inner self
style in your dress
confidence in your walk
guidance in your advice
secrets in your tears
cuteness in your laughter
warmth in your heart
pureness in your soul
&
your love by your side.

When World's Collide

She lived in the clouds
He was down to earth

She was brand new
He was used

She'd seen many faces
He'd met many souls

She was fine china
He was porcelain

She was the sun
He was the moon

She was living
He was surviving

She lived in vibrant colours
He was black & white

She owned time
He made the most of the time he had

She was a warm summer's day
He was the harshness of winter

She needed him
He was waiting for her

She looked to shape the future
He was shaped by the past

She was poetry
He was rap

She was a princess
He needed saving

She was sunshine
He was rain

Together, they were a rainbow.

Pain Perseverance Promise

Yesterday was filled with pain
wounded memories inexorably influential
poor judgements and misplaced trust
limiting your true potential.

Today is filled with perseverance
facing the challenges of life
trying to appreciate the little things
as you try to strive through strife.

Tomorrow will be full of promise
each moment a chance to improve
your self, your life, your future
a life which only you need to approve.

Querencia

I walked into the lost & found today to see what I could find
I'd lost so much over the years I wasn't sure what was mine.
As I looked around the place I could see things old and new
One step in and a connection immediately grew.

Trust in a jar; hope hanging by a thread
Stories of the heart collecting dust as they sit unread.
A cracked mirror with a reflection of someone who looked familiar
Hard drives of different versions labelled 'please forgive us'.

I run my fingers across a globe of lost and forgotten places
Memories and embraces lie on the floor on ripped out pages.
In a corner a temple where prayers are yet to be answered
Eternal happiness which never took flight because they remain anchored.

Whispers of wishes fly across the ceiling like shooting stars
The limitless ambitions can be seen through the wall's cracks & scars.
Plans and goals semi flourished in bottles and vases
All the luck of life in a deck of cards full of aces.

It goes on, it's never ending, it's got the whole kit and caboodle
There's even a roller-coaster of emotions, what makes us truly human.
Clocks with fixed times from moments that were hoped would last forever
The lights, harnessing the mind's power, they will go out never.

A piano with keys made of promises; some kept and others broken
A lyrical sheet with loving words that still remain unspoken.
Priceless memories relived as, on screen, they replay
Stacks of oxygen tanks from when breaths were taken away.

A shield made of love, to protect from all forms of destruction
Blueprints of a better life, semi complete and under construction.
As I delve deeper into the abyss I begin to feel whole
Like it's all an extension of me, a configuration of my soul.

A guiding light enlightens me and makes the house known
I've finally found what I had lost; I am now home.

Printed in Great Britain
by Amazon